DISCONNECTED

PORTIA INGRAM

Mind Align Solutions , LLC

New York

Disconnected: Why You Feel Busy But Aren't Moving Forward

ISBN: 979-8-9877049-3-6

Printed in the United States of America
First Edition
Publisher: Mind Align Solutions, LLC

This book is intended for informational and educational purposes only. It does not constitute medical, psychological, or legal advice. Readers should consult appropriate professionals where necessary. The author is not responsible for any actions taken based on the information presented in this book.

TABLE OF CONTENTS

Grounding

Take a deep breath.

If you're anything like the young adults I've spoken to over the past few years— the students, the entrepreneurs, the creatives, and the professionals just starting out—that deep breath might be one of the few truly present moments you've had all day.

You feel busy, right? You're consuming information at an explosive rate. You know all the latest trends, the political debates, the successful morning routines of entrepreneurs three continents away, and the exact steps to optimize your life. You have access to every piece of self-improvement content ever created.

Yet, despite this flood of knowledge, sometimes it feels like you're standing still. You're working hard but not actually making progress toward the goals that matter most to you. You feel anxious, scattered, and often find yourself scrolling right through the exact window of time you'd planned to use for meaningful work, only to feel guilty afterward.

The problem isn't laziness, and it isn't lack of information. The problem is digital noise, and it's creating a dangerous disconnect.

We live in a world designed to capture your attention and keep it fragmented. This constant exposure to online personalities, endless opinions, and perfectly curated lifestyles is doing more than just distracting you—it's destabilizing your sense of self.

The core truth of this book is simple: When your identity is scattered across a thousand feeds and opinions, you lose the ability to be present. And if you can't be present, you sever the vital connection to the most important person in your life: your Future Self.

That Future Self—the person you are striving to become, the one who possesses the life, skills, and discipline you aim for—is not just a fantasy. It is your ultimate psychological guide, the engine of your long-term success, and the source of true, intrinsic motivation.

This book is about understanding how the digital world weakens the link between who you are now and who you want to be later.

We'll explore the science—from the foundational role of presence to the surprising way your mirror neurons are being hijacked—and give you the tools to stop consuming content about success and start actually creating it.

It's time to move beyond superficial productivity and reclaim the intentionality that will build the future you deserve.

Let's Work!

We just lightly explored the idea of how the day-to-day digital noise we face impacts our concept of self and therefore our Future Self. The following exercises will help you understand how you see your future and what is keeping you from being present.

Reflection Questions

Who do you imagine yourself becoming? Think about who you'd want to be one year from now.

_____

_____

_____

What emotions arise when you think about your Future Self?

_____

_____

_____

When was the last time you felt fully present?

_____

_____

_____

Action Exercise
Digital Noise Inventory

List 5 sources of digital noise in your daily life and how they impact your focus or identity.

1. _____

2. _____

3. _____

4. _____

5. _____

Application Challenge

For the next 24 hours, practice a 5-second pause before opening any social app. Write down what you notice.

_____

_____

_____

_____

_____

_____

_____

_____

_____

_____

Future Self Alignment Check

Does your current daily routine support the person you want to become? Why or why not?

_____

_____

_____

_____

_____

_____

_____

_____

_____

_____

Chapter 1

The Scattering Effect
(Why Presence is Your Superpower)

We used to think of our identity as relatively solid, forged through real-world trial and error. Now, identity is fluid, constantly being tested, tweaked, and sometimes shattered, by the relentless influx of the feed.

Every time you open the app, you are given a new, perfect persona to try on: the disciplined student, the minimalist travel blogger, the finance guru, the hyper-confident artist. This creates what I call The Scattering Effect: your focus, your energy, and your sense of who you are supposed to be are scattered across dozens of incompatible ideals.

When you're constantly shifting between identities, you forget that the most powerful force for change is presence.

Presence is the ability to anchor your thoughts, feelings, and energy to the current moment. It's where decisions are made, habits are built, and real learning happens. If you are always living one half-step in the past (revisiting an embarrassing post) or one half-step in the future (planning the perfect caption), you are not here.

And if you are never here, you cannot build a reliable sense of you.

Think of presence as the soil in which your Future Self grows. If the soil is weak, contaminated by the digital noise of comparison and distraction, nothing meaningful can take root.

The key steps you need to take right now—studying for an exam, writing that business plan, having a tough conversation—require 100% of the present you. Without that focus, your efforts are diluted, and your ability to connect with long-term goals fades away.

Let's Work!

Chapter 1 explains how identity becomes scattered by digital personas and comparison loops. The exercises in this section help you understand the impact of trying on identities on your feelings of authenticity.

Reflection Questions

Which online identities influence you the most, and why?

_____

_____

_____

What personas do you try on without realizing it?

_____

_____

_____

How has comparison shaped your choices in the last month?

_____

_____

_____

Reflection Questions Cont..

What parts of you feel strongest and most authentic?

_____

_____

_____

_____

_____

Where do you feel your sense of self becoming fragmented?

_____

_____

_____

_____

_____

Exercise
Identity Map

Think about 3 influencers or accounts you follow most often and write down what you believe they value based on their content.

_____

_____

_____

_____

What Do YOU Value?

_____

_____

_____

_____

_____

_____

Identity Map Cont..

Step 2: Complete the Venn Diagram

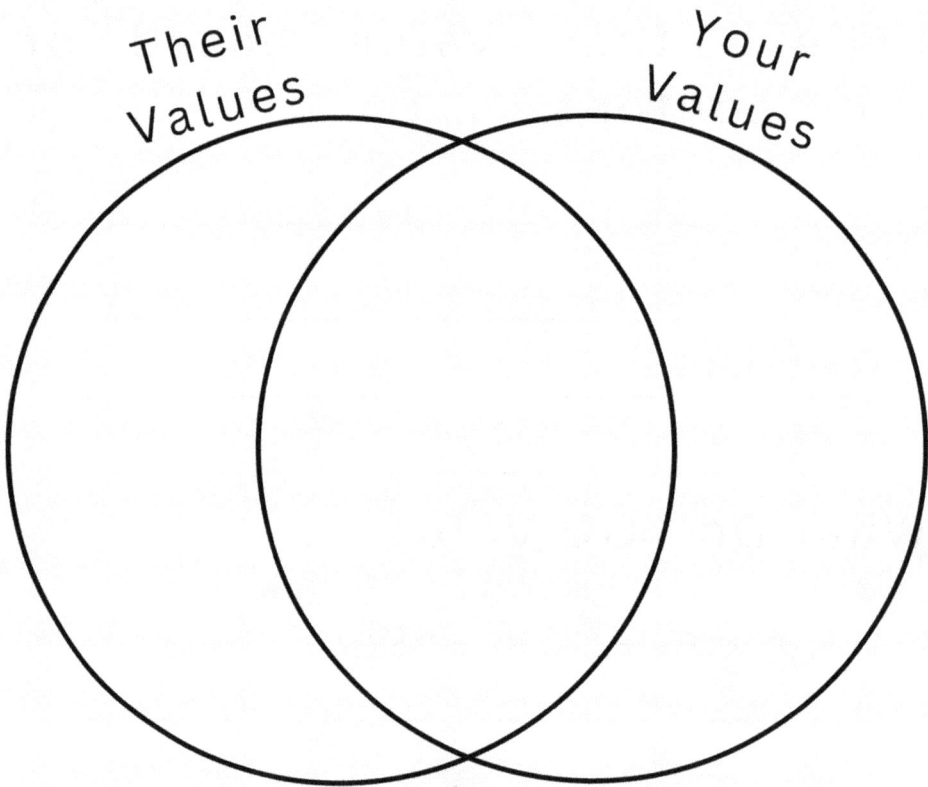

Their Values

Your Values

Put what overlaps here
[This is where your consumption aligns with your authentic self]

Application Challenge

Choose one digital identity (influencer or account) you will consciously stop comparing yourself to for one week.

_____

_____

_____

Future Self Alignment Check

Is the identity you're maintaining online consistent with the life you want to build offline?

_____

_____

_____

_____

_____

_____

_____

_____

_____

_____

Chapter 2

Meet Your Co-Pilot

The concept of the "Future Self" isn't abstract motivation speak; it's hard psychology. Research, notably from Hal Hershfield, shows that we often treat our future selves like strangers. When looking at a photo-aged version of themselves, people showed similar brain activity as when looking at a picture of a celebrity or another unrelated person.

This matters profoundly.

If you feel disconnected from the person you will become—if that Future You feels like a stranger—why would you sacrifice instant gratification?

The scrolling. The sugary snacks. Let's not talk about letting go of procrastination. Could you cut down on or cut out these things for Future You's benefit? You are far more likely to save money, exercise, or study for a difficult test if you feel a strong empathetic connection to the person who will benefit from those sacrifices.

Your Future Self is your psychological GPS. When the connection is strong, the Future Self acts as a guide, providing intrinsic motivation. You don't need an external reward system because the reward is the gradual achievement of becoming that person. This connection forces you to ask: "Is the choice I am making right now serving the person I want to be twelve months from now?" However, when digital noise compromises your presence, this feedback loop breaks down. You become highly susceptible to temporal discounting—the psychological phenomenon where we value immediate rewards far more than future rewards.

A weak connection to your Future Self means you'll always choose the instant dopamine hit of a notification over the slow, difficult work required to achieve long-term success. You simply cannot see the point of sacrificing, because the benefactor (Future You) feels too foreign and far away.

Let's Work!

Chapter 2 reframed presence as a tool for self-regulation. The following exercises are there to help you understand if you are spending most of your time living in the past, running towards the future or responding consciously in the present.

Reflection Questions

When do you feel most present in your body and mind?

_____

_____

_____

What distractions pull you away from the moment most often?

_____

_____

_____

How does your lack of presence affect your progress?

_____

_____

_____

Reflection Questions Cont..

What do you think your life would look like with 20% more presence each day?

_____

_____

_____

What choices in your life require more presence?

_____

_____

_____

_____

_____

_____

Guided Exercise
The Grounding Moment

Complete 5 rounds of intentional breathing:
Step 1) Inhale 4 seconds

Step 2) Hold 2 seconds

Step 3) Exhale 6 seconds

Application Challenge
Practice this 2-minute grounding exercise anytime you feel overwhelmed this week.

Future Self Alignment Check

Consider how having a greater sense of presence could strengthen your relationship with Future You?

_____

_____

_____

_____

_____

_____

_____

_____

_____

Exercise
Presence Anchor

Choose a physical or sensory anchor (touching your heart, breath, a phrase). Write it below and how you'll use it.

My Presence Anchor:

_____

_____

Chapter 3

The Productivity Hijack

This is where brain science gets tricky—and where social media truly maximizes its hold on us. Our brains are equipped with mirror neurons (MNs). These remarkable cells fire both when we perform an action and when we observe someone else performing that same action. They are the biological foundation of empathy, learning, and imitation.

How did you learn to tie your shoes or ride a bike? Your MNs were busy translating observation into potential action. In the physical world, MNs are powerful teachers. In the digital world, they are easily hijacked.

Consider this scenario: You watch a 15-minute video of a hyper-successful creator meticulously organizing their workspace, planning their week, and drinking a perfect green smoothie. While watching, your mirror neurons are firing. Your brain registers the activity as if you are performing the virtuous, disciplined action.

The result? You receive a small, satisfying hit of dopamine and a feeling of pseudo-productivity. You feel motivated, informed, and even slightly exhausted—as if you actually did the work.

This is the Productivity Illusion: Feeling like you are "doing the work" simply by consuming content about success, wellness, or productivity. You spend an hour watching a tutorial on building a profitable side hustle, and your brain tells you, "Great job! We worked on the side hustle today!" But you didn't actually open a spreadsheet, write a single line of code, or contact a single client.

This illusion is insidious because it replaces genuine, effortful action with passive consumption, leading to a corrosive cycle:

X *Consumption: You feel motivated by watching someone else succeed (MNs fire).*
X *Reward: Your brain releases dopamine, reinforcing the watching behavior.*
X *Inaction: Since the reward was already received, the motivation to actually get up and execute the task disappears.*

The digital noise is weaponizing your

fundamental biological structures, convincing you that passive learning is the same as active building. It's time to break that cycle by forcing your mirror neurons to fire for actual, present self-initiated effort.

Let's Works!

Chapter 3 went over how mirror neurons (MNs) create the illusion of productivity by rewarding observation instead of action. These next exercises will help you apply what you learned from the chapter so that you'll discover if you're spending valuable time living in the Productivity Illusion or executing goals in real life.

Reflection Questions

What types of content do you consume the most?

_____

_____

_____

How does your body feel after a long scroll session?

_____

_____

_____

What tasks or goals do you find yourself not executing because you are doing more consuming than creating?

_____

_____

_____

Exercise
Mirror Neuron Awareness Log

Track moments you feel productive after watching someone else's productivity. Be sure to include who you were watching and what they were doing.

_____

_____

_____

_____

_____

_____

_____

_____

_____

Application Challenge

For the next 3 days, whenever you open an app, say silently or out loud:
"Am I here to consume or create?"
- If you're consuming - set a timer for 8 minutes
- If creating - name your task in one sentence before you begin

Future Self Alignment Check

Honest Moment- After reading the previous chapters and performing the exercises: Were your mirror neurons trained toward watching or doing?

_____

_____

_____

_____

Chapter 4

From Consumption To Creation

To build the future you want, you must shift your energy from content consumption to goal creation. This requires strengthening the presence-Future Self-connection and teaching your mirror neurons to reward action, not observation.

Here are a few strategies to rebuild that vital feedback loop:

1)*The Time Travel Exercise: Making the Future Self Real*

The Hirschfield research shows that making the Future Self clearer increases motivation. So basically..

You need to make Future You less of a stranger.

Action Step: Dedicate 20 minutes to deeply visualizing your ideal self 10 years from now. Don't just list achievements; use sensory details. What does Future You smell like (coffee, books, fresh air)? What does their desk feel like (wood, metal, clean)? What specific problems are they solving?

The Power of Clarity: Once established, post a physical reminder of Future You near your workspace. When you are tempted by distraction, visually reference that anchor and ask: "Is this scroll serving Future Me?"

2)The Action Audit: Identifying the False Reward

We must identify where our mirror neurons are being duped.

Action Step: Use the "Conversion Rule." This means that for every hour of consumption related to a specific goal, you must dedicate at least 30 minutes to active implementation of one specific takeaway. Did you watch a video on budgeting? You must open your bank app and set up a budget tracker before watching the next video. This forces your MNs to fire for action.

3) The 5-Minute Rule: Lowering the Activation Energy

The biggest hurdle is the activation energy required to start a task.

Your brain will always prefer the ease of scrolling over the difficulty of starting.

Action Step: If a task feels too big (e.g., "Write a chapter of my book" or "Clean the entire garage"), shrink it down to five minutes of effort. Your goal is not to finish, but merely to start.

Why it Works: Once you are physically engaged in the task—your hands are typing, or you are holding the vacuum —your mirror neurons and other brain systems shift from passive observation to active engagement. The momentum gained in those first five minutes usually carries you far beyond the initial self-imposed limit, strengthening the feedback loop that says:

Real Action = Progress

Exercise
Digital Boundary Blueprint

Write 3 rules for your tech use that
protect your mental space.

1)

_____

_____

_____

2)

_____

_____

_____

3)

_____

_____

_____

Guided Exercise
The 90-Day Future Self Commitment

Write a commitment letter (on paper or on a digital device you refer to often) outlining what you will focus on for the next 90 days.
Include your desired outcomes and:
- Habits to build
- Habits to release
- Support systems
- Daily non-negotiables

Choose **one** thing to work on each day.

Future Self Alignment Check
Commitment Statement

Complete the sentence:
I commit to becoming the version of myself who...

_____

_____

Final Chapter

The Power of Intentional Living

You are not doomed to be a passive consumer of information. You have the power to select what enters your attention span and what guides your choices.

The journey from Disconnected to Intentional begins with one conscious choice: to prioritize the present moment and strengthen your empathy for the person you are actively building.

By understanding the mechanics of distraction, reclaiming your presence, and purposefully directing your motivation, you can align your daily actions and energy with the magnificent Future Self currently waiting for you. Stop watching others build their lives. Start building yours.

The Future You depends on it.

Final Reflection Questions

What part of your identity shifted the most while completing this workbook?

_____

_____

_____

What habit or thought pattern will you carry forward from here?

_____

_____

_____

How has your relationship with your future self evolved?

_____

_____

_____

NOTES

NOTES

_____

_____

_____

_____

_____

_____

_____

_____

_____

_____

_____

_____

References

Future Self Psychology

Hershfield, H. E. (2011). Future self-continuity: How conceptions of the future self transform intertemporal choice. Annals of the New York Academy of Sciences, 1235(1),30–43. https://doi.org/10.1111/j.1749-6632.2011.06201.x

Hershfield, H. E., Goldstein, D. G., Sharpe, W. F., Fox, J., Yeykelis, L., Carstensen, L. L., & Bailenson, J. N. (2011). Increasing saving behavior through age-progressed renderings of the future self. Journal of Marketing Research,48(SPL),S23–S37. https://doi.org/10.1509/jmkr.48.SPL.S23

References Cont..

Mirror Neurons

Rizzolatti, G., & Craighero, L. (2004). The mirror-neuron system. Annual Review of Neuroscience, 27, 169–192. https://doi.org/10.1146/annurev.neuro.27.070203.144230

Iacoboni, M. (2009). Imitation, empathy, and mirror neurons. Annual Review of Psychology,60,653–670. https://doi.org/10.1146/annurev.psych.60.110707.163604

Temporal Discounting /
Why We Choose Now Over Later

Frederick, S., Loewenstein, G., & O'Donoghue, T. (2002). Time discounting and time preference: A critical review. Journal of Economic Literature, 40(2), 351–401. https://doi.org/10.1257/002205102320161311

www.ingramcontent.com/pod-product-compliance
Lightning Source LLC
Chambersburg PA
CBHW081141090426
42736CB00018B/3442